Francis Marion

The Swamp Fox

Colonial Leaders

Lord Baltimore
English Politician and Colonist

Benjamin Banneker
American Mathematician and Astronomer

Sir William Berkeley
Governor of Virginia

William Bradford
Governor of Plymouth Colony

Jonathan Edwards
Colonial Religious Leader

Benjamin Franklin
American Statesman, Scientist, and Writer

Anne Hutchinson
Religious Leader

Cotton Mather
Author, Clergyman, and Scholar

Increase Mather
Clergyman and Scholar

James Oglethorpe
Humanitarian and Soldier

William Penn
Founder of Democracy

Sir Walter Raleigh
English Explorer and Author

Caesar Rodney
American Patriot

John Smith
English Explorer and Colonist

Miles Standish
Plymouth Colony Leader

Peter Stuyvesant
Dutch Military Leader

George Whitefield
Clergyman and Scholar

Roger Williams
Founder of Rhode Island

John Winthrop
Politician and Statesman

John Peter Zenger
Free Press Advocate

Revolutionary War Leaders

John Adams
Second U.S. President

Samuel Adams
Patriot

Ethan Allen
Revolutionary Hero

Benedict Arnold
Traitor to the Cause

John Burgoyne
British General

George Rogers Clark
American General

Lord Cornwallis
British General

Thomas Gage
British General

King George III
English Monarch

Nathanael Greene
Military Leader

Nathan Hale
Revolutionary Hero

Alexander Hamilton
First U.S. Secretary of the Treasury

John Hancock
President of the Continental Congress

Patrick Henry
American Statesman and Speaker

William Howe
British General

John Jay
First Chief Justice of the Supreme Court

Thomas Jefferson
Author of the Declaration of Independence

John Paul Jones
Father of the U.S. Navy

Thaddeus Kosciuszko
Polish General and Patriot

Lafayette
French Freedom Fighter

James Madison
Father of the Constitution

Francis Marion
The Swamp Fox

James Monroe
American Statesman

Thomas Paine
Political Writer

Molly Pitcher
Heroine

Paul Revere
American Patriot

Betsy Ross
American Patriot

Baron Von Steuben
American General

George Washington
First U.S. President

Anthony Wayne
American General

Famous Figures of the Civil War Era

John Brown
Abolitionist

Jefferson Davis
Confederate President

Frederick Douglass
Abolitionist and Author

Stephen A. Douglas
Champion of the Union

David Farragut
Union Admiral

Ulysses S. Grant
Military Leader and President

Stonewall Jackson
Confederate General

Joseph E. Johnston
Confederate General

Robert E. Lee
Confederate General

Abraham Lincoln
Civil War President

George Gordon Meade
Union General

George McClellan
Union General

William Henry Seward
Senator and Statesman

Philip Sheridan
Union General

William Sherman
Union General

Edwin Stanton
Secretary of War

Harriet Beecher Stowe
Author of Uncle Tom's Cabin

James Ewell Brown Stuart
Confederate General

Sojourner Truth
Abolitionist, Suffragist, and Preacher

Harriet Tubman
Leader of the Underground Railroad

Francis Marion

The Swamp Fox

Kay Cornelius

Arthur M. Schlesinger, jr.
Senior Consulting Editor

Chelsea House Publishers

Philadelphia

Produced by 21st Century Publishing and Communications, Inc.
New York, NY. http://www.21cpc.com

CHELSEA HOUSE PUBLISHERS
Production Manager Pamela Loos
Art Director Sara Davis
Director of Photography Judy L. Hasday
Managing Editor James D. Gallagher
Senior Production Editor J. Christopher Higgins

Staff for *FRANCIS MARION*
Project Editor/Publishing Coordinator Jim McAvoy
Project Editor Anne Hill
Associate Art Director Takeshi Takahashi
Series Design Keith Trego

The Chelsea House World Wide Web address is
http://www.chelseahouse.com

3 5 7 9 8 6 4 2

Library of Congress Cataloging-in-Publication Data

Cornelius, Kay.
    Francis Marion / Kay Cornelius.
      p. cm. — (Revolutionary War Leaders)
    Includes bibliographical references (p.) and index.
    ISBN 0-7910-5976-6 (hc) — 0-7910-6134-5 (pbk.)
    1. Marion, Francis, 1732-1795—Juvenile literature. 2. Generals—
United States—Biography—Juvenile literature. 3. South Carolina—
Militia—Biography—Juvenile literature. 4. United States—History—
Revolution, 1775-1783—Biography—Juvenile literature. 5. South
Carolina—History—Revolution, 1775-1783—Juvenile literature.
[1. Marion, Francis, 1732-1795. 2. Generals 3. United States—
History—Revolution, 1775-1783—Biography. 4. South Carolina—
History—Revolution, 1775-1783.] I. Title. II. Series.
E207.M3 C67 2000
973.3'092
[B]   00-038383
                                                           CIP

Publisher's Note: In Colonial and Revolutionary War America, there were no standard rules for spelling, punctuation, capitalization, or grammar. Some of the quotations that appear in the Colonial Leaders and Revolutionary War Leaders series come from original documents and letters written during this time in history. Original quotations reflect writing inconsistencies of the period.

Contents

As a youth, Francis Marion spent many happy hours in his boat, exploring the South Carolina swamps and bayous.

"Swamp Boy"

More than 100 years before the American Revolution, in the 1600s, people started coming to live in the British colony of South Carolina. It was named for King Charles I of Great Britain. (*Carolina* comes from the Latin word for Charles.) The main port was first called Charles Towne, then Charleston.

Among those early settlers was a French family who wanted to worship God in their own way. Gabriel Marion came from Rochelle, France, and took up land along the marshy coast on Goose Creek near Charleston. The rice grew well there.

His son, also named Gabriel, built a rice **plantation** called Goatfield, near Georgetown. Young Gabriel married Charlotte Corde and started to raise a family of his own. The couple had four sons and a daughter. Then, in 1732, their last child was born. Few records were kept in those days, and no one knows the exact date or place of this baby boy's birth.

Perhaps in honor of his grandfather's home country, the boy was named Francis. He was both the youngest and the smallest of the Marion children. But his small size did not keep Francis in the house. From a very early age he liked to be outdoors. He loved to explore the **swamps** and marshes around the plantation. Cattails and reeds grew along the edge of the swamps, but to get deep into its heart, he had to use a boat. In a small boat called a **pirogue**, carved from a cypress tree, Francis could go deep into the swamps' narrow streams and quiet wetlands.

No place on earth smells like a swamp. Even

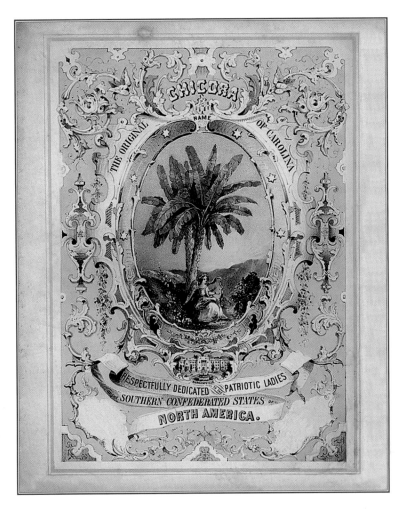

A drawing of the original seal of South Carolina, featuring a palmetto tree in its center.

if he had been blindfolded and led there, Francis could tell exactly where he was just by taking a deep breath. There was the smell of moldy, always damp earth, of course. But many plants also lived in the swamps' warm, moist air. Some were beautiful, like the wild azaleas and blue flags and white water lilies. Others, like comfrey and bindweed, were used as a cure for fevers and other diseases.

Wetlands occur when an ocean or river floods into low-lying land, and the water does not drain out. Swamps are usually always wet, but higher land inside a swamp may stay dry part or most of the time. The water can be several feet deep in some places. Dead-looking pine and cypress trees can be found in most swamps and Spanish moss drapes many trees.

All kinds of creatures lived in or near the swamps, and young Francis grew to know them well. He heard the call of the owls, and saw deer, raccoons, and wild turkeys. He admired the herons—graceful, long-legged, long-beaked birds who looked for their food in the wetlands and marsh grasses. In the streams that fed the swamps, Francis often saw the knobby head of an alligator as it silently swam away from him. Snakes sometimes hung down from the old cypress trees. They looked so much like the vines twisting around the trees that they were hard to see. The snakes and alligators made many people afraid to go into the swamps.

Francis was not afraid of the strange world of the swamps. Sometimes he hunted or fished. Sometimes he just watched the animals and listened to the calls of the birds. He probably enjoyed having some peaceful time away from his noisy house full of older siblings. But no matter how far he went into the small side streams and creeks that fed the **bayous**, Francis never got lost.

When he was not out in his beloved swamps, Francis spent some time studying. He did not have to leave his own house to be taught. In those days, planters usually hired teachers to come and stay in the house. One room would be made into a classroom. Almost every day, the children would have lessons in arithmetic, spelling, and reading.

They wrote using quill pens made from the feathers of a fat goose. They had to dip the sharp

Francis learned to write using a quill pen and a pot of ink, much like the ones shown here.

point of the quill into a bottle of black ink every time they wanted to make a letter. They had to be careful not to spill the ink or drop any of it onto their paper. They also had lessons in drawing and music.

We do not know how many years of schooling

Francis and his brothers and sister had, but their lessons came to an end when their father died. Their happy days at Goatfield Plantation were over.

The family went to live at Belle Isle, a plantation owned by Francis's oldest brother, Gabriel. It was a much smaller place than Goatfield. Francis missed his old home. Perhaps he did not like his brother telling him what to do either. By the time he turned 15, Francis was beginning to feel restless. He still loved the swamps and spent time there whenever he could, but he also wanted to see more of the world.

Francis had visited the port of Charleston. The white-sailed merchant ships that sailed into and out of that harbor must have been a beautiful sight. These ships brought many kinds of goods from faraway places all over the world. The ships' cargo—what they carried—was worth a lot of money. Pirates often tried to get aboard the ships before they reached Charleston. Once on the ships, the pirates would take away the spices, fine silks, gold and silver coins, or anything else of value they could find.

Francis had heard about these pirates, but he did not fear them. He knew that ocean storms were dangerous to even the largest ships, but he did not fear the storms either. The teenager still wanted to go to sea.

Finally, his older brother Gabriel took him to Charleston. Francis was too young and too small to be a regular sailor, but a coastal schooner bound for the West Indies needed a ship's boy, and the captain agreed to take him on board. A schooner was a small sailing ship with two masts—one on the front and one on the back of the ship. Coastal schooners had that name because they followed the coastline some distance away from the land.

Francis knew that the West Indies islands were a source of molasses, spices, and other valuable trade goods. No doubt he expected he would see new, strange sights when he arrived.

Francis had heard exciting tales of pirates and their ships. But his first sea voyage was marred by a shipwreck and nearly a week adrift in a small boat, and he decided he never wanted to go to sea again.

After about a week at sea, the voyage came to a sudden end. The crew spotted a large group of whales in the ocean. Francis was probably excited when he first saw the unusual sight, but then he may have realized how dangerous the whales could be to a ship and its crew. The largest of all sea creatures, these whales kept coming closer and closer. Finally they swam under the schooner and then came up to the surface of the water.

The whales' huge heads hit the bottom of the ship. The boards of the deck broke with a cracking sound. Water poured in quickly. Everyone knew the ship was going down and would sink soon. Francis and several other crew members were able to get into the ship's small "jolly boat" and escape. But they had no time to take anything to eat or drink with them.

For six days they drifted, going nowhere. Hungry sharks swam all around the small boat. The sun baked them by day, while the nights were very cold. A passing rain shower helped give them some much needed water, but Francis knew he was growing weaker every day. His great sea adventure had not turned out the way he had hoped. He must have wondered if he would ever see dry land again.

Finally a passing ship saw the tiny boat and rescued the shipwrecked survivors. Francis had lived through those terrible days, but he was left sick and weak. He went back to Belle Isle to rest and get stronger.

He would still take his pirogue into the swamps, but from then on, Francis never wanted to be a sailor or to go to sea again.

Francis loved Belle Isle, and most especially Hampton Hill, his favorite part of the plantation. After receiving Hampton Hill as a gift from his brother, Francis decided to manage the land well and someday build his own home there.

Farmer and Fighter

After his short career as a sailor, Francis Marion returned to Belle Isle to get his strength back and help out around the plantation. A few years later, his brother Gabriel had a surprise for him. Gabriel offered Francis a part of the plantation called Hampton Hill.

The offer pleased Francis very much. He had hoped someday to have a place of his own. But he realized that it might be years before he could afford one. He already knew and loved Hampton Hill, his favorite part of Belle Isle. Yet it would be a man's job to see that the land was worked the right way. He would have to see to it that all the field hands did what they should. Could he do it?

Francis felt a little uncertain at first, but he was even more excited that at last he would be on his own. And in a few years, he should have enough money to build a home there and ask Mary Videau to marry him. Mary lived on a much larger plantation. They had been friends since childhood, but Francis wanted to succeed at managing Hampton Hill before he asked her to be his wife and leave her lovely home. So Francis settled down to grow rice.

As a matter of course, he joined the South Carolina **militia** in 1761. This service as a part-time soldier was something almost all men in the colonies did. They kept their own weapons ready in case of an emergency in the area. They met from time to time with others from the same area. The militiamen learned basic military drills and practiced firing their guns.

Francis's first taste of battle came when he and his men were asked to fight Cherokee Indians who were attacking settlers in North and South

Militiamen fight off an attack by Native Americans. Francis fought in many skirmishes like this one during the French and Indian War.

Carolina. Conflict with Indians was part of a larger war that raged between Great Britain and France in the colonies. Both nations claimed lands in North America, and from 1754 to 1763, they struggled for control of the American colonies in what is called the French and Indian War.

For years, the French had tried to get groups of Native Americans to fight for them. The French hoped that if settlers in British colonies were attacked, they would give up and leave America. Then the French could take over the land. During the war, some Native Americans sided with the French, while others fought alongside British soldiers and colonial militiamen.

In fighting the Cherokees, Francis and the other militiamen learned some valuable lessons. They saw how the Native Americans fought, which was quite different from the way the regular military units were used to fighting.

In Europe at that time, war was like a game played with a set of rules. But the Cherokees did not follow any of Europe's formal rules. They moved quietly and quickly through the woods and gave no warning before they attacked. Their arrows were silent and could be used in damp weather. The British soldiers used guns, which in those days took a long time to load and shoot. The guns also were very noisy and could not be fired in the rain.

Although British soldiers and militiamen fought together in the French and Indian War, the British regular army did not have a high opinion of the colonial militiamen. They thought the militiamen were **undisciplined**. The British soldiers wore bright red jackets and marched into battle in rows as Europeans had been doing for many years. They looked like professional soldiers.

The militiamen did not have fancy uniforms and did not march side by side into battle. Often they would split up and surprise an enemy. They did not look as professional as the British army, but the militiamen had something more important on their side: their new way of fighting.

Still, serving as a militiaman often meant being away from home for long periods. What they really wanted was to see to the needs of their homes and families. That was why some men left the militia after only a few days or weeks of fighting. They would often go home to plant or harvest crops. Then, after they had attended to matters at home, they went back to their units.

British general Thomas Gage points at his troops marching in the background. Francis and other colonial militiamen didn't march in rows but hid in the forest and surprised their enemies.

These men would fight to defend their homes and the land around them. But they did not want to march any great distances to fight the enemy.

Francis did not leave the militia very often to see to his land. As a result, when he returned home from fighting, he found that his fields were in a terrible state of **neglect**. And he had missed Mary Videau very much. So when he got home, the first thing he did was go to see Mary. This time, he decided there was something important he had to do–he asked her to marry him.

Mary agreed, but there was one problem: her mother was not in very good health. Mary felt she could not leave her sick mother alone. Francis was disappointed. But he knew that Mary had a duty to take care of her mother, just as he had a duty to serve with the militia. So Francis told Mary he would build a house for her and wait until the time came when they could be married.

At that time, Francis was not sure how long it would be before he was again called into service. The end of the French and Indian War had brought problems for Great Britain, even though it had won the war. Many of these problems would directly affect the colonists and their ties to Great Britain. Like many other colonists, Francis feared that one day, there could be a war between the colonies and their British rulers.

American colonists hoist a tax collector up a pole called a "liberty tree." Anger at the taxes imposed by Great Britain pushed the colonists toward rebellion.

3

The Colonies
Go to War

It is easy to think that the American Revolution began on July 4, 1776. On that day, the Declaration of Independence was made public. In it, the authors declared that the American colonies would no longer be a part of Great Britain but rather an independent nation. The people who put together and signed the Declaration of Independence represented all the British colonies in America, from Massachusetts to Georgia. They did not like being told what to do by a government on the other side of the Atlantic Ocean. They said it was time for the Americans to do things their way.

In reality, the problems that the colonists had with the British really started quite a long time before that July day in 1776. One of the biggest causes of their problems had to do with money.

The American colonies were doing well. But Great Britain was in **debt** after many years of war with France. To get money to pay its debt, Great Britain decided to make all colonists pay taxes on things like tea and paint. These were things that the colonists could not grow or did not make themselves and thus needed to import.

When the British started to tax these and other items, people living in the colonies said it was not fair. They were British citizens, but they were not allowed to have any say in the way they were ruled. It seemed time for the colonies to get together to decide what to do. South Carolina sent representatives to meet with people from other colonies to discuss how they were going to deal with the British

Colonists often gathered in taverns like this, where they could read newspaper accounts of the latest British taxes and argue about either fighting Great Britain or remaining loyal.

government and these new taxes.

What to do about British rule was a subject that most everyone in the colonies was talking about. Many colonists hoped that the British would change their minds and wished that the king would give them a chance to say how they thought they should be ruled. But others began to believe that they would need to fight for their freedom.

In South Carolina, many people were divided in their loyalties. Not everyone wanted to be free of Great Britain. Some people still had many relatives and friends in England and thought of that country as their home. Some even sent their children across the ocean to go to school there.

But the families of many other colonists had been in America for so many generations that they no longer felt close ties with the mother country. And some families, like Francis's, had not even come from England in the first place.

By the 1770s, many of the colonists were angry at having to pay British taxes. Some had begun to connect these taxes with a much larger issue: liberty. They wanted the freedom to make their own rules. These people were first known as **Whigs.** After the Revolutionary War started, they were sometimes called rebels or **patriots**.

The eastern part of South Carolina, the coastal area where Francis lived, had rich soil and was called the low country. The farmers in that area mostly grew rice and indigo, a plant that was used to make blue dye. They had a great deal of land, owned slaves, and had a good income.

Inland, the area called the up country, was different. There, the soil was not as rich and the farms were quite small. Most of the farmers were very poor. They could

Rice and indigo were the two crops that helped make South Carolina a rich colony by the 1760s. In those days, all the colors in cotton, linen, and wool clothes came from dyes that were made from plants. Indigo is used to make beautiful dark blue dye.

Indigo was not a crop native to South Carolina. But a teenaged girl named Eliza Lucas Pinckney decided to grow it. She lived on a plantation near Charleston. In 1744, after five years of trying, she grew a good crop of indigo. She shared her seeds with others, and soon indigo became a major crop in South Carolina.

Indigo plants being processed. Both the colonists and the British depended on indigo for dyeing clothes. It was an important cash crop for South Carolina's plantation owners.

not afford to buy many of the goods that came into Charleston from Great Britain. So they did not care if taxes were put on things that they could not buy. They did not like it that the rich planters from the coast ran the colonial government. Most of the people who lived in the up country stayed loyal to England and were called **Tories** or Loyalists.

Beginning in 1775, Francis served in the South Carolina Provincial Congress. Along with most of the other planters there, he voted for war against the British. The same year, South Carolina raised two **regiments** of soldiers to fight in the Revolutionary War. Francis became a captain in the Second Regiment.

He was rapidly promoted to lieutenant colonel. But the man who was later called a true hero of the American Revolution did not look very heroic. He was barely five feet tall and was not what most people would think of as handsome. From a few sketches and portraits we know he had a large forehead and a calm and steady look in his face. His dark eyes seemed to be able to look right through people. Although he did not look the part of a military leader, he always proved himself in battle.

Francis spent a great deal of his time training and disciplining his troops. Many of them were not used to bathing or even wearing shoes. Francis wanted his men to be well trained, to look neat and tidy—and most of all, to obey orders.

All of this training would pay off when the British forces began fighting in South Carolina. The British needed to control the port of Charleston so that they could bring in their supplies. And they also did not want other countries to send goods to help the rebel colonists. In June 1776, British warships tried to take the

In June 1776, the British sent nine ships to capture Charleston Harbor. Francis and other soldiers were stationed at a small fort (later called Fort Moultrie) on Sullivan's Island in Charleston Harbor. From there, they could see the enemy fleet approaching.

The fort had been built with logs made from the very thick trunks of native **palmetto** trees. The British cannon balls could not break through the tough wood. Finally the British gave up and left. Because the palmetto trees helped to save the fort, South Carolina was nicknamed "the Palmetto State," and the palmetto tree is on the state flag.

The battle at Charleston, where British ships tried to take the harbor. Francis and his men successfully drove the ships away.

city. Francis and his men fought bravely against them in the Battle of Fort Moultrie and succeeded in driving the British ships away.

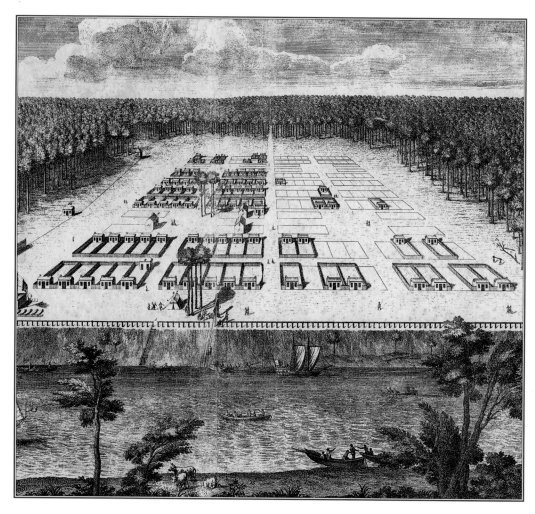

A plan of Savannah, Georgia, a town surrounded
by forests and a river. After many small battles,
the British took control of the port there.

About 25,000 South Carolinians fought in the
Revolutionary War. There were also many small
battles that broke out in South Carolina between

groups of Loyalists and patriots. Then, in 1777, the British soldiers took Savannah, a port in Georgia not far from South Carolina. The British position there was too strong for the colonists to attack.

For several years, the South Carolina colonial troops had no battles to fight, but Francis tried to keep his men disciplined and together. He wanted them to stay alert and be ready to fight when they were needed.

Then, Francis had an unfortunate accident that changed everything.

Francis (on horseback, third from right) leads his men across a river. Francis's main camp was on an island surrounded by creeks and a river.

Marion's Brigade

In 1780, things looked bad for all the men who had been fighting on the American side of the war. Lord Charles Cornwallis, a British general, entered South Carolina with many troops. In March, they laid siege to Charleston. Francis and some soldiers were at a party in a house in Charleston. Francis tried to leave by a second-story porch. In the darkness, he could not tell how far down the ground was. He jumped anyway and hurt his ankle so badly that he could hardly walk. He got away but was forced to go back to his home on the Pee Dee River to let his ankle heal.

Only a few days later, the British took Charleston. They captured most of the other American troops and their officers there. The Second Regiment no longer existed.

After Francis heard of the fall of Charleston, he and some of his men hid in the swamps to avoid being captured by the British. In early summer, he and a few other rebels went to North Carolina. There, they linked up with the American general Horatio Gates, who had raised an army and was going to bring it into South Carolina to fight the British.

But the general had little use for Francis's ragtag band, which did not even have proper uniforms. Instead of letting them join his troops, Gates sent the men out as scouts. Francis and his men would rather have marched with Gates, but it was lucky that they did not. Gates's troops went into South Carolina, but they were defeated very badly by the British at a place called Camden.

Once again, Francis returned home. He then

General Charles Cornwallis, who commanded all British troops in the South. He later surrendered at Yorktown, marking the end of the Revolutionary War.

formed a small group of fighting men. Under Francis's command, they had gone into hiding around the swamps. Soon the men became known as "Marion's **Brigade**." Francis made his headquarters deep in the swamp on Snow's

Island. It was a low ridge about five miles long and two miles wide. Three creeks and the Pee Dee River flowed all around the island. It was a remote place that very few people had ever seen.

By late August 1780, Marion's Brigade felt they were ready and started attacking the British. They would come out of the swamps to surprise and attack passing British troops. Then they would disappear into the swamps again, as quickly as they had appeared. This kind of fighting is called **guerrilla warfare**, and Francis turned out to be a genius at it.

He had a few experienced officers, but most of the men were volunteers who came and went as they pleased. Sometimes he had 200 or more men with him. At other times, he commanded only 20 or 30. They had no uniforms and no one to give them supplies. They often captured British wagons to get food and ammunition. Many of the men even rode into battle without guns. Some carried swords they made from sawmill blades.

The men's horses were the most important

things they owned. Francis knew if his men could not move fast after a raid, they would be captured. The members of Marion's Brigade did not have an easy life. They longed for salt to make the wild game they killed taste better. Often they had little food besides sweet potatoes. Sometimes the bad water in the swamps made them very sick. Francis tried to stay healthy by drinking a mixture of vinegar and water.

In many army units, the commanders lived much better than their troops. This was not the case with Francis. He shared his men's hardships. The officers usually had only one shirt. Francis kept using the leather helmet of the Second Brigade even after it had fallen into a campfire and been partly burned, and he slept on the ground, wrapped in a single blanket. He walked with a limp because the ankle he hurt in Charleston never completely healed. Yet he was able to outwit the British time after time.

One of Francis's more unusual victories happened at a place called Fort Watson. He wanted

After the British captured Charleston in 1780, they were in control of all of South Carolina.

to attack the fort but had no cannon. In only one night, he and his men built a tall log tower overlooking the fort. In the morning they were in a position to fire down into the fort. The deadly small-arms fire was too much for the British inside, and they surrendered.

After a raid on Georgetown in spring 1781, Francis finally was able to put on a regimental uniform. Before then, he wore a short, red jacket. The men wore white feathers in their hats so everyone would know they were not Tories.

Francis used scouts to find out where the British were and how many men they had. Also, farmers and others in an area often gave him valuable information about the movements of the British. He kept his own plans secret. He learned many tricks, like covering a bridge with blankets so his horses' hooves would not make any sounds that might warn the enemy.

Redcoats, as British soldiers were called, made fun of the colonists. The tune "Yankee Doodle" was meant to insult them. They called the colonists "Yankees," and a "doodle" was a half-wit. The British sang the song when they marched to Lexington and Concord.

When they retreated, the story goes that the colonists sang it back to them as a taunt: "Yankee Doodle went to London, riding on a pony. He stuck a feather in his hat and called it macaroni."

Many rebel soldiers, including Francis, put feathers in their hats. "Macaroni" was a British slang word for "dandy," or someone who dresses in the latest fashion.

Francis liked to move out of the swamps at dusk and ride all night. Sometimes, he and his men rode as much as 70 miles with only a brief stop for a quick meal. Other times, he would wake his men before the sun came up. They liked to ride into a place where British soldiers had camped for the night and were sleeping. Then they would make off with the food and rifles before the enemy soldiers woke up and knew what was happening. Francis's actions were small, but they had big results. The British had to use many soldiers to guard roads and supply trains or they could not get food and gunpowder to their troops.

On August 20, 1780, Francis, with only 16 men under his command, attacked a British column. They were able to free 150 American prisoners. Then he and his men escaped back into the swamps. When the British tried to follow them without knowing where they were going, their horses sank deep into the mud.

"We'll never find that cursed Swamp Fox," said the British commander, a man named Tarleton. From then on, the man who had

Francis and his men at his headquarters. Many times, Marion's Brigade outwitted the British and returned to hide in the swamps.

grown up as a "swamp boy" was known as the Swamp Fox.

Many stories have been told about Francis and the brave and bold things he did. One of the tales has a famous painting to go with it. Artist

A famous painting of Francis sharing his dinner of sweet potatoes with a British officer.

John Blake White called it *General Marion Inviting a British Officer to Share His Meal.*

According to the story, a British officer was invited to visit Francis's swamp camp under a flag of **truce**. The general offered his visitor a sweet potato baked in the coals of the campfire and served on a slab of pine bark.

"But, General, surely this can not be your

usual fare," the British officer said.

"Indeed, sir, it is," said Francis, "and we are fortunate on this occasion, entertaining company, to have more than our usual fare."

When the British officer returned to Georgetown, his colonel asked why he looked so serious.

"I have cause, sir," said he, "to look serious."

"What! Did Marion refuse to speak with you?"

"No, sir."

"Well, then, has old Washington defeated Sir Henry Clinton, and broke up our army?"

"No, sir, not that but worse."

"Ah! what can be worse?"

"Why, sir, I have seen an American general and his officers, without pay, and almost without clothes, living on roots and drinking water; and all for liberty! What chance have we against such men!"

The story goes on to say that the officer resigned from the British army and went back to England.

Time after time, Francis and his men would come charging out of swamp or forest to defeat surprised British forces.

Riding with Marion

Marion's Brigade fought the British troops that had been sent to put down the rebellion in South Carolina. But sometimes they also had to fight back when Tory Loyalists came after them. A man named Ganey, who had been an officer in the South Carolina militia, formed a Loyalist regiment to operate in the same area as Francis's men. Many of these recruits had never been in a military unit before. They knew nothing about drilling and obeying orders. But when Ganey sent out a call, more than 250 men volunteered.

Ganey planned to take Francis by surprise and break

up his unit. Before daylight on a fine September morning, he and 45 of his men rode toward a place where they knew Francis was camped. The remainder of the more than 250 men, led by a captain named Barefield, followed on foot. They looked forward to capturing the Swamp Fox.

But Francis sent out patrols day and night. He had heard about the Tory army the day before. He knew they would come after him and his men. At that time he had only 53 men with him. The Tories had almost five times more men. Winning a fight against such odds might seem hopeless. But Francis knew that if he surprised the enemy, he could win. He told no one of his plan. Before dawn he woke up his men, and they rode out in search of the enemy.

Two hours later, an advance guard rode back and told Francis that the road ahead was blocked by the 45 armed men. An eager young man named James, in Francis's command, enthusiastically shouted for his men to follow him as he rode after Ganey. The Tory band quickly scattered, and James chased Ganey. James had not looked back and did not know that his men were not following him. Soon he came to the thicket where Ganey and a few of his men had hidden. It was at that moment that James realized his men were not behind him and he was all alone.

The young militiaman was in great danger, but he thought fast and acted quickly. As if he were addressing many men, James shouted back over his shoulder, "Come on my boys! Come on! Here they are!"

Without waiting to see how many men were coming, Ganey and his men turned and retreated through the forest. In the confusion of their hasty retreat, no one thought to send word back to the infantry troops led by Barefield, who were behind them. Only 15 men from Ganey's group escaped. The other 30 were wounded or killed.

Francis learned from a captured Tory that the more than 200 other men, who were on foot, were only about three miles away. Ten minutes later, they found the enemy. A scout had informed the Tory captain that Francis's men were coming. Barefield formed his men into a battle line and they stood waiting, **muskets** ready.

With his 50 men against more than 200 Tory fighters, Francis knew it would not be wise to try a charge straight in. He pretended that he was afraid and ordered his men to pull back. They retreated a distance and then stopped and hid in woods and brush surrounding an open area. There, Francis and his men waited for Barefield to march right into their **ambush**.

The Tories thought they were in no danger. They were completely surprised when more of Francis's men came charging out from the trees, yelling and firing their weapons. Many of Barefield's men managed to fire only one volley. But with no mounted men to protect them while they reloaded, the only thing they could do was to run and hide in the woods and the Little Pee Dee Swamp.

Francis's men rode slowly along the edge of the swamp and dared the Loyalists to come out.

A painting of Francis and his men in action. In reality, the troops did not have fine uniforms and often were without food and other supplies.

They did not, and Francis called his men off and left the scene. He found out that most of the men had gone into hiding in their homes. The Tory brigade that had wanted to catch the Swamp Fox fell apart. Francis had seen to it that there would be no Tory uprising.

As an extra bonus, 60 of the men who had earlier left Francis's brigade rejoined the group. The British helped Francis recruit even more men, although they did not mean to do it. The British commander in the area decided he needed to give horses to more of his soldiers. Playing a trick, he called together the planters in the area and told them the British were there to rescue them from the rebels. While he spoke, his men stole all the planters' horses. Many of those who attended that meeting had to walk home. But as soon as they could get another horse, they joined Francis's brigade to fight back.

The fighting continued. One British commander reported that he had burned over 50 homes and plantations. He was proud that he had killed many sheep and cattle. But he also admitted that he needed more help in keeping

Francis and others like him under control.

Francis could not provide his men with everything the British had. But many times he was able to do a great deal with the little that he had. One of the men he worked with was Lieutenant Colonel Henry "Lighthorse Harry" Lee. One day they were trying to capture a plantation house that the British had made into a fortress. The British inside knew that reinforcements were on the way, and they thought their defenses were good enough to keep the rebels out. With time running out before more British troops got there, Lee and Francis made a decision. They would set the house on fire to make the British leave.

Mrs. Rebecca Motte owned the large house in which the British were staying. She had been forced to leave her home and was living in a nearby cabin. The rebels were going to use fire arrows like the Indians, she was told. The roof shingles were dry and would catch fire easily. The British would have to get out, and Francis and Lee would be ready for them. Mrs. Motte

A woman and her family set fire to their wheat crop. Many colonists were willing to destroy their property to help stop the British.

agreed that her home had to be burned. "If it were a palace, it should go," she said. Then she saw the rather crude bow and arrows they were going to use. She went back inside her cabin, brought out a much better bow, and offered it to the men.

Under a white flag of truce, the rebels gave the British commander one last chance to surrender. He would not. At noon, flaming arrows were sent onto the dry roof shingles. It is said that the bow was pulled by a private from Marion's Brigade whose own home and farm had been burned out by the British. Those inside the house tried to put out the fires, but an hour later, they hung out the white flag. Only two men from Marion's Brigade had been killed. Inside the house they found food and other necessary supplies. That night, Mrs. Motte gave a dinner for the officers of both armies.

The American author William Cullen Bryant (1794–1878) was only a baby when Francis died. But he liked the stories about the Swamp Fox so much that he wrote a ballad, or song, about Francis and his men, which can be sung to the tune of "Yankee Doodle Dandy."

> Our band is few, but true and tried,
> Our leader frank and bold;
> The British soldier trembles
> When Marion's name is told.
> Our fortress is the good green wood,
> Our tent the cypress tree;
> We know the forest round us
> As seamen know the sea.
> We know its walls of thorny vines,
> Its glades of reedy grass;
> Its safe and silent islands
> Within the dark morass.

After many discouraging defeats, in 1780, the Americans turned the tide in the South with their victory against the British at the Battle of Cowpens.

6

Victory
at Last

The Revolutionary War lasted for six long
years. During that time, 137 battles were
fought in South Carolina—more than in any other
colony. Of these battles, 103 were fought by South
Carolinians alone, without the help of any other
colonies.

As the years passed with no end to the war in
sight, Francis sometimes became discouraged. His
men had been left to take care of themselves,
almost always having to get their own supplies.
There were times when Francis felt extremely
unhappy. Perhaps he was so sad because he and

Mary Videau had not gotten married before he became so completely swept up in the war. He did not think that anyone cared about the difficult life that he and his men had taken on for the sake of winning America's freedom. Yet through it all, Francis stayed in the field, leading his men.

"Will the war never end?" It was a question that everyone on both sides of the war must have asked many times through the long years of battles, victories, and defeats.

Then things really began to look up for the Americans. On October 7, 1780, the patriots won a very important battle at Kings Mountain. A total of more than 1,000 British troops were killed, wounded, or captured by the Americans in that confrontation. At the beginning of the next year, American general Daniel Morgan and his men won another great victory at a place called Cowpens.

After their defeat at the Battle of Cowpens, the determined British turned the tide again

At the Battle of Eutaw Springs, Francis lost many brave fighting men, but the Americans finally won the battle.

and chased the American army into the North Carolina colony. Cornwallis fought General Nathanael Greene there at a place called Guilford Courthouse in March 1781.

Marion's Brigade continued to cut British supply lines in the South. On May 29, 1781, they took the town of Georgetown without firing a single shot. The British had heard that Francis and his men were coming, and they quickly left before the brigade arrived.

In August, Francis and General Greene met the last remaining large British force in America at a place called Eutaw Springs. It was by far the biggest battle Francis's men had ever seen. Although the Americans won, Francis lost many of his men. He was ordered to gather his men together once again and be ready to fight the British forces one more time if Cornwallis tried to retreat through South Carolina.

But in October, Cornwallis surrendered to the Americans after the bloody Battle of Yorktown. For the first time in many years, Francis, the man who had lived much of his life in the swamps, was free to return home.

Not much of it was left. His plantation was only a mile from a major roadway where the

General Nathanael Greene led American troops in the South in many victories over the British.

British had marched many times. His cattle had all been driven off, his horses had been stolen, and his house had been burned to the ground.

A Southern plantation house. After the war, Francis returned home to rebuild his neglected and ruined plantation.

His entire plantation was in absolute ruins. So Francis began to rebuild it.

During the war, Francis had served in the army for many hard years without receiving any pay. After the war, Francis continued serving South Carolina as a senator. In spite of all he had been through, he still opposed a bill that would have taken the property of former enemies.

He also continued to command a military brigade until 1794. The United States Senate awarded him a gold medal "as a mark of public **approbation** for his great, glorious, and meritorious conduct." He was also promoted to full colonel in the **Continental** army on September 30, 1793.

In all the long years they had been apart, Francis had not forgotten Mary Videau. The war had been over for some time and his plantation had been rebuilt. On April 20, 1786, Francis and Mary were finally married. They had no children of their own, but the couple adopted a grand-nephew, Francis Marion Dwight.

The Swamp Fox could not forget the years he had spent leading his men through the swamps. Occasionally, he and Mary would return to those areas. Sometimes he visited soldiers who had been with him. They enjoyed talking about the adventures they had shared.

Loved and honored by the men with whom he had fought, Francis died on his plantation on February 27, 1795, at the age of 63. He was buried at Belle Island Plantation, home of his brother Gabriel. His grave is in present-day Berkley County about 10 miles west of St. Stephen. His own plantation was about 15 miles upriver and is now under the waters of Lake Marion.

Inscribed in the marble stone over his grave are these words: "Francis Marion . . . Who lived without fear, and died without reproach."

It is fitting that the Swamp Fox should be laid to rest near the swamps he first explored as a child,

To the people of South Carolina, Francis was a hero, the Robin Hood of the Revolution. But his name might have been forgotten if not for one man.

Parson Mason Locke Weems wrote a book in 1809, *The Life Extraordinary of General Francis Marion*, which tells many stories about Francis and his men. Some of the facts came from a man who served with Francis. In some of the stories, Weems stretched the truth a little bit. And sometimes, he even made things up entirely. Weems's book helped to turn the Swamp Fox into a legendary figure.

fought in as a soldier, and always loved.

Reminders of Francis are still everywhere. Stories are told about the Swamp Fox's brave deeds, and his name lives on as well. In South Carolina, "Marion" appears in the names of schools, a lake, a county, a town, and a national forest. But his name can also be found in many other places in the country. Soldiers who served in the American Revolution were given land for their service. They moved down into the South, up into the Midwest, and out into the West. As they settled and built new towns, they honored the Swamp Fox by giving his name to many of these places. Today, at least 17 counties and 19 towns bear the name of Marion.

To this day, people along the Ashley River, near the coast, still talk about a big tree called the Marion Oak, near Bacon's Bridge. Francis's men often camped there when they guarded the bridge to keep it out of British hands. Many years later, a man named William Henry Johnson took pictures of that huge old oak tree, draped with Spanish moss.

Some people say if you go deep into the swamps today and are very quiet and close your eyes, you might hear something.

Is that sound just the wind blowing through the Spanish moss in the cypress trees? Or might these places really remember the Swamp Fox and whisper stories about him and his men?

GLOSSARY

ambush–a surprise attack on an enemy by people in hiding

approbation–approval

bayou–a marshy area of still water on a creek or stream

brigade–a large group of soldiers

Continental–term for a soldier of the American colonies during the Revolutionary War

debt–money owed to someone

guerrilla warfare–military operations that rely on surprise and are carried out by a small group

militia–group of volunteers in an area who meet to drill and protect or defend their land

musket–a type of shoulder gun with a long barrel

neglect–to fail to take care of or pay proper attention to someone or something

palmetto–a kind of palm tree with leaves on the very top; its wood is very thick

patriot–a person who loves and is willing to fight for his country, as the American colonists did during the Revolutionary War

pirogue (pronounced pi–ROHG)–a small boat shaped like a canoe

plantation–a large area where a particular crop or crops are grown, typically in the South

regiment–a military unit

swamp–wetlands that occur in a low, flat area such as a coastal plain where water rushes in during high tides but does not run out

Tory–a person in the American colonies who remained loyal to the king of England during the American Revolution

truce–an agreement between enemies to stop fighting for a time, usually so the commanders can talk to each other

undisciplined–lacking self-control or the ability to operate as a unit

Whig–one name for a supporter of the patriots' cause during the American Revolution

CHRONOLOGY

1732	Born Francis Marion at Goatfield Plantation in St. John Berkley Parish (County), South Carolina.
1747	Goes to sea; is shipwrecked; returns to his brother's planation at Belle Isle.
1761	Joins the South Carolina militia; fights with the British against the Cherokee Indians; is promoted to lieutenant colonel; learns new fighting techniques from the Cherokee Indians.
1775	Elected to South Carolina Provincial Congress and votes to go to war against Great Britain; becomes captain in South Carolina's Second Regiment.
1776	Takes part in Battle of Fort Moultrie; defends the city of Charleston and its harbor against the British.
1777	The British capture Savannah, a port in Georgia not far from South Carolina.
1779	Becomes senior field officer in South Carolina.
1780	British general Lord Cornwallis brings troops into South Carolina; Francis injures his ankle escaping from the British; returns home and forms Marion's Brigade.
1781	American army takes over Georgetown from the British in May; Cornwallis surrenders at Yorktown in October; Francis returns home.

1786   Marries Mary Videau.

1788   South Carolina becomes America's eighth state.

1793   Is promoted to colonel in the Continental army.

1795   Dies on February 27 in South Carolina.

REVOLUTIONARY WAR TIME LINE ═══

1765 The Stamp Act is passed by the British. Violent protests against it break out in the colonies.

1766 Britain ends the Stamp Act.

1767 Britain passes a law that taxes glass, painter's lead, paper, and tea in the colonies.

1770 Five colonists are killed by British soldiers in the Boston Massacre.

1773 People are angry about the taxes on tea. They throw boxes of tea from ships in Boston Harbor into the water. It ruins the tea. The event is called the Boston Tea Party.

1774 The British pass laws to punish Boston for the Boston Tea Party. They close Boston Harbor. Leaders in the colonies meet to plan a response to these actions.

1775 The Battles of Lexington and Concord begin the American Revolution.

1776 The Declaration of Independence is signed. France and Spain give money to help the Americans fight Britain. Nathan Hale is captured by the British. He is charged with being a spy and is executed.

1777 Leaders choose a flag for America. The American troops win some important battles over the British. General Washington and his troops spend a very cold, hungry winter in Valley Forge.

1778 France sends ships to help the Americans win the war. The British are forced to leave Philadelphia.

1779 French ships head back to France. The French support the Americans in other ways.

1780 Americans discover that Benedict Arnold is a traitor. He escapes to the British. Major battles take place in North and South Carolina.

1781 The British surrender at Yorktown.

1783 A peace treaty is signed in France. British troops leave New York.

1787 The U.S. Constitution is written. Delaware becomes the first state in the Union.

1789 George Washington becomes the first president. John Adams is vice president.

FURTHER READING

Bodie, Idella. *The Revolutionary Swamp Fox.* Orangeburg, S.C.: Sandlapper Publishing, 1999.

——. *The Secret Message: Heroes and Heroines of the American Revolution.* Orangeburg, S.C.: Sandlapper Publishing, 1998.

Brown, Marion Marsh. *The Swamp Fox.* Philadelphia: Westminster Press, 1992.

Fradin, Dennis Brindell. *South Carolina.* Chicago: Children's Press, 1992.

Freeden, Charles. *South Carolina.* Minneapolis, Minn.: Lerner Publications, 1991.

Thompson, Kathleen. *South Carolina.* Austin, Tex.: Raintree Steck-Vaughn Publishers, 1996.

INDEX

PICTURE CREDITS

page

3: National Archives
6: New Millennium Images
9: The Library of Congress
12: New Millennium Images
15: New Millennium Images
18: New Millennium Images
21: The Library of Congress
24: The Library of Congress
26: National Archives
29: The Library of Congress
32: The Library of Congress
35: National Archives
36: The Library of Congress
38: National Archives
41: The Library of Congress
44: The Library of Congress
47: National Archives
48: National Archives
50: New Millennium Images
55: The Library of Congress
58: National Archives
60: National Archives
63: National Archives
65: National Archives
66: The Library of Congress

ABOUT THE AUTHOR

Former English teacher **KAY CORNELIUS** lives in Huntsville, Alabama. She has written magazine articles, short stories, one novella, and nine novels. She likes to study and write about history. *Francis Marion* is her third children's book. She enjoyed writing it because one of her ancestors actually rode with the Swamp Fox.

Senior Consulting Editor **ARTHUR M. SCHLESINGER, JR.** is the leading American historian of our time. He won the Pulitzer Prize for his book *The Age of Jackson* (1945), and again for *A Thousand Days* (1965). This chronicle of the Kennedy Administration also won a National Book Award. He has written many other books, including a multi-volume series, *The Age of Roosevelt.* Professor Schlesinger is the Albert Schweitzer Professor of the Humanities at the City University of New York, and has been involved in several other Chelsea House projects, including the COLONIAL LEADERS series of biographies on the most prominent figures of early American history.